OPERATION UNICORN

MAKING **POSSIBLE** THE **IMPOSSIBLE** IN 2021

CATHERINE BRUNO

ARCHWAY
PUBLISHING

Archway Publishing books may be ordered through booksellers or by contacting:

Archway Publishing
1663 Liberty Drive
Bloomington, IN 47403
www.archwaypublishing.com
844-669-3957

Interior Image Credit: Hagan Family

Scripture taken from the King James Version of the Bible.

ISBN: 978-1-6657-1262-0 (sc)
ISBN: 978-1-6657-1263-7 (e)

Library of Congress Control Number: 2021919375

Print information available on the last page.

Archway Publishing rev. date: 09/29/2021

DEDICATION

To my wonderful father, James Michael Hagan, for showing me how I had the potential to be a unicorn rather than a mess.

To the Ladies of the Fork and their fifteen-year plus friendship for which I will always be grateful. I have had each of these ladies choose a pseudonym in this book to protect their and their families' privacy, but I want to assure you that they are all very real and wonderful ladies in our world today. As they have chosen to name themselves, the full group consists of: Sophia Edwards, Grace Potter, Marsha Gables, Sawyer Reynolds, Bonnie Ice, Bea Sky, and Judith Mackenzie.

To J. R. Huey for growing into a literary woman and for allowing me to write copious letters to her over the summer of 2020, and in spite of the demands of her life, writing me back two wonderfully long letters on the status of what her family was up to in the summer of 2020.

To the staff at the Hiawatha Public Library in the summer of 2020 for helping me to untangle my dark and twisty thoughts and for tolerating my copious letters and cards. A special nod to M. P., who gave me Uni, pictured on the front, and inspired me to start *Operation Unicorn* even before I realized how much I would need it.

To Tracy Clair and Iris Williams (name changed to protect her privacy) for helping me put my adult and childhood experiences in perspective.

To Brenda Jurgensemeier for helping me come to a personal understanding of what being a unicorn meant to me.

My personal definition of unicorn: anything or anyone that shows impossible strength in impossible circumstances.

Save me from the lion's mouth, for thou hast heard me from the horns of the unicorns. (Psalm 22:21 KJV)

In honor of Edward Hagan,
a poor Irish farmer who had
the good sense to love his son,
I return the love to Iowa.

CONTENTS

ACKNOWLEDGMENTS

To my grandma Phyllis Miller for showing me how to be the good wife and approving of Mr. Bruno when I asked her thoughts about him. The yellow roses you have planted in my heart will never stop blooming.

To my cousin Patrice Caraway for giving me the courage to publish by publishing her own book, having four beautiful children, and rising to the challenge of life and love like a true unicorn.

To Uncle Mark and Aunt Loretta Miller for showing me I could do good things with my artwork, how to love my mother-in-law, encouraging me to write, and raising three wonderful children, including Kara Rose, my favorite.

To my cousin Mary Hagan for being brave and kind enough to send a younger high school cousin encouragement mail while visiting Europe in the summer of 2006.

To the Ave Regina girls for helping me rediscover Christ in Catholicism. I strongly believe if it had not been for your timely influence in my life in college, I would not be a strong Christian woman today.

To Aaron Paul Barkey (now with the Lord) and his parents for showing me how to be an incredible special needs teacher through the experience and wisdom they imparted to me when and after I worked for them.

To my uncle Ned (Edward) Hagan for being the Edward (Ned) Hagan who lived to be a happy old man, never let me lose at checkers, and taught me that no matter what your job is, you can always be happy.

To my aunt Corinne Kelly for teaching me that I can do a large amount of good even if my physical size is small.

To my aunt Emilie Hagan for teaching me to empathize with all people no matter their size, helping me when I needed it, and teaching me how to be an Irish fairy.

To Sally and Abraham (names changed because they are young) for having the courage to love and get married in 2020.

To my husband, David, for loving me in all seasons of our lives. I hope and pray we will grow old enough together that our hair will be white, and we can "more officially" be Mr. and Mrs. Santa Claus at Christmas.

To my Moms Club friends for being there for me and allowing me to be there for them. It has been an absolute joy watching our kids grow up together and supporting each other through it all.

To Regan Smetz for reteaching me some of life's basic lessons when I forgot them, and for having the kindness and patience to hope I would understand.

To the good women in Titus II at our church, no matter the season of your life, know you are in my prayers. I thank you all for the wisdom and love you have shown me, young and old alike.

To my high school librarian Shirley Sharma for showing me what a difference a kind librarian can make in a kid's life and showing me how to be "very particular" about watching my bank account. Sharma is the only woman I ever remember catching our bank on a mistake they made. Her good use of her particularness showed me how to use my own for good.

To Roisin Delaney and Heather Spangler for being incredible Little Free Pantry and charity advocates. I could not be prouder or happier that you good women live in our community.

To the Plummers and the Lovetinskys for their lifelong family friendships.

To Autumn Plummer for rebaptizing me and never showing me anything but a fierce purple loyalty.

To Rachel and then Josie at Simon and Schuster for being wonderfully positive when they interacted with me via e-mail in the process of publishing this book and writing my post-derecho adventures.

To my cousin Ted Crowley for bringing Martin Hagan's quarantine comments in the *Wichita Beacon* to light this year and sharing them with the Hagan family.

To my grandmother Josephine Hagan, now with the Lord, for teaching me how to love and care for people with special needs via her impeccable care of my aunt Mary Jo.

CHAPTER **ONE**

AN IRISH UNICORN

Jerry Donovan, an Irish immigrant to America, who was known to blow a lot and tell fairy tales and other stories, would say, "Ned Hagan came from a fart in Ireland where the sun never shone and the potatoes never grew."

His friend Edward "Ned" Hagan, also an Irish immigrant to America, was wont to reply, "From my bedroom window at home in Ireland, I could see the sun rise out of the ocean every morning."

Once upon a time in Independence, Iowa, a farmer by the name of Edward Hagan lost all but three members of his family. Three sons lived. The rest of the family was buried in St. John's Cemetery. As a young boy, my great-grandfather, Martin Hagan, was orphaned. He and his two brothers walked out into the world alone but alive. Martin Hagan walked several miles and was offered a job at a farm for a lot of money. But the farmer was not John Casey. Edward Hagan, his father, had said, "Go to work for John Casey." So Martin kept walking.

When he finally came to John Casey's home, both John and his wife agreed they couldn't afford to take him on. After Martin explained that his father had specifically requested it, and he had nowhere else in the world to go that might feel like home, John and his wife gave Martin a job as a farmhand. And as the years went on, John Casey became like a father to Martin.

As Martin grew older, he grew restless. He met a family named Kelly and played baseball with their boys. He went to Tifford's Collegiate Academy in Vinton, Iowa. It took him eight years to graduate because he only went to school in the winter (October through April). Board, room, and tuition were fifty dollars a term. Then he was drafted for the Spanish-American War. He was sent to Cuba after the fighting was over.

Martin then entered the University of Iowa's medical school. No premed education was required. He paid for medical school via a government bill similar to the more recent GI Bill. After two years there, he realized that clinical opportunities in Iowa City were very limited, so he transferred to Northwestern University in Chicago for big-city clinical opportunities.

The pressure of his studies got to him at one point, and he was approaching burnout or breakdown.

Fortunately, one of his professors counseled him on how to work through it. His problem was described to him as neurasthenia (nervous exhaustion). At the time it was thought to be caused by exhaustion of the nerve cells, and it required a long recovery period. He stayed with that explanation. Today they consider the cause to be emotional.

Years passed. The Kelly boys he'd played baseball with grew up. Their younger sister, Kathryn Kelly, grew up and became a teacher in Iowa. When Martin met Kathryn as an adult, he slowly fell in love. When he finished his fellowship, he married Kathryn.

The head doctors asked each other, "What about this man Hagan?" One doctor was from Chicago, Illinois. The other was from Wichita, Kansas, a boondock town if ever there was one. Doctor Fab, the one from Wichita, said, "If you don't take him, I will." And so Martin and Kathryn Hagan moved to Wichita for a medical job for Martin. They settled in town and had thirteen children. An infant named Edward "Ned" Hagan, after Martin's father, died at birth. My grandfather, Francis Hagan, lived despite being a sickly child. His brother Tom was never his favorite, as Tom had once "accidentally" put a pie in his face by means of a revolving door into the kitchen.

Due to the irony of life, these same brothers ended up settling in Wichita, becoming doctors themselves, and raising their children together—seven for Frances and five for Tom. Tom and Ann had four boys and one girl, Kathryn. When Mary Kathryn Hagan was five years old, she died quite suddenly from a hole in her heart. The whole Hagan family grieved. And years later, when I was a child, I wondered who the little girl in the picture was with half my name for I was named Catherine Hagan.

The Hiawatha Public Library in Hiawatha, Iowa, where I volunteered, took my eldest to story time, and worked until the birth of my second child. Before the COVID lockdown, I would take my second child to story time too. I currently donate to the Little Free Pantry, which they host, and am blessed that they can provide my family and me with books and crafts.

I wrote the following letter to the staff at the Hiawatha Public Library in the middle of the summer of 2020, after giving them several Dunkin' Donuts gift cards and encouragement cards and making frequent donations to the Little Free Pantry.

Dear library folk,

I've been meaning to write y'all a letter so you understand why I'm doing what I'm doing with y'all. And, I suppose, there's no time like the present.

I am currently thirty-five years old.
Last year my good friend and elementary
and high school classmate Patty Wilson
posted a small autobiography of Chaplain
Emil Kapaun—the man our high school
was named after—on Facebook. Chaplain
Kapaun died in a modern war when he was
thirty-five years old.

As a high-schooler, I had heard stories
about him and always thought that he died
when he was middle-aged or much older
than me. I was shocked that I was now the
same age as Kapaun when he died.

Kapaun saved many lives during the
war. He was a POW and was eventually
taken by enemy soldiers to die in a hospital when they could find an excuse to get
rid of the man who kept their other prison-
ers of war's spirits up too much.

I am, if anything, a dark and twisty
woman who has experienced many things
in my relatively short but eventful life of
thirty-five years. Our family, right now, is
blessed to be in a better position than so
many others. My husband has an excellent
job, and our boys and I are healthy.

I often believe I became a Bruno, rather
than a Hagan, marrying my husband to survive. Brunos, like Big Russell Bruno, whom

our eldest is named after, are incredibly ornery and *thrive* in challenging circumstances. Big Russell Bruno parachuted out of aircraft carriers in army tanks during World War II and lived to tell the tale. When he was ninety years old he went to meet the Lord, passing away in the arms of his beloved wife of sixty years, Doretta Bruno.

After my husband proposed to me after a bad tornado, he took me to visit his grandparents, Russell and Doretta, again. I went out to check on the garden with my husband's sister Laura, and Big Russell said, I quote, "I really like that girl!" My then fiancé spilled the news to him: "Grandpa, I'm going to marry that girl." I walked back in from the garden to find them laughing in joy with their arms around each other. My fiancé happily let me know the full story later.

I would also like to cite my great-uncle Martin Hagan in all this. He was, I believe, the best mentor for a teacher I've ever met. He, when his hair was gray and balding, would walk on his treadmill and memorize the names of his students with their pictures so he could say hi to them in the halls with their names and make sure they knew they existed and were *important*.

Last, but certainly not least, my good mother, Sharon Hagan, named me "Catherine" after a librarian whom she always had peanut butter parfaits with at Dairy Queen in Parsons, Kansas, when she, my mother, was working her first elementary school teaching position.

Sincerely,
Catherine Marie Hagan Bruno

The following is a Facebook conversation with my good friend Sally Smith on July 28, 2020, after I asked what food was in the boxes they gave away via HACAP in the Hiawatha City Hall parking lot. I wanted to know what the food was so I could post recipes for people who needed them as so many of my friends were asking for recipes using the split peas, dried garbanzo beans, and rice that they received in these boxes.

Sally: If you are wanting recipes google the ingredients you have and the recipes. You will come up with all kinds of ideas.

Me: Lol, no Sally. We're blessed fiscally during these strange times BUT I've seen a lot of bean or split pea donations to the little free pantries which I patronize and was trying to get a feel for what was going on or not going on there. We live in strange times but thank you for your wonderful letter of encouragement!!!!!

Sally had sent me a typed letter within a gorgeous bejeweled blue-and-green card describing the best gifts she had ever received and the best teacher she had ever had. The best teacher she ever had, after tears from a very young Sally, had pulled Sally's dolly back up out of the outhouse toilet after Sally had dropped it there while she was at school. As Sally wrote, "Now that's commitment!"

> Sally: You are welcome. I am always searching for recipes. That is why I do not get anything done. Stay Safe!!!

A July 29, 2020, Facebook conversation with Sally:

> Me: Please check your front porch, and let me know if Uni missed your house by one or not …

> Sally: Nothing on the porch.

> Me: (unicorn emoji) will be back … what's your house number?

> Sally: Found it on neighbor's porch. Told him I wasn't stealing off his porch. LOL Thanks so much for goodies.

CHAPTER TWO

A SUMMER CURVEBALL

I Facebook messaged my good friend Jacque (a woman wiser and more experienced than I) after I received a call from my mother that my father's lymphatic cancer had returned, and he was going to be undergoing chemo three times a week for it. I was suffering in trying to process these facts in a healthy manner amid the social constraints of the COVID-19 pandemic.

> Me: I had my first crying breakdown yesterday. It involved a strong discussion with David [my husband], a lot of therapeutic swinging on our swing set outside, and well, therapeutic crafting to recover …
>
> Jacque: Hugs, my friend! I've spent more time crying than not this last week. Life is

just really, really hard sometimes! Thank you for all my little "surprises." [heart emoji]

I had gifted her little baskets of flowers and unicorn trinkets and ribbon and soap, the results of my therapeutic crafting. I dropped them off on her front porch, rang the doorbell, and ran off.

My friend Shari, after seeing my many comments about unicorns on Facebook, posted that she was thoroughly confused and had no idea what I was talking about. Shari wanted to know what the deal was with unicorns and me, so she posted a question on one my unicorn posts: "What's going on with you and unicorns? I missed something. I'm so confused."

Via a private Facebook message, I sent her a picture of Uni the Unicorn, shown on the front of this book, with the explanation of how Marta Petermann, adult reading program coordinator at the Hiawatha Public Library, had given her to me as a reward for their adult summer reading program.

Shari: I remember that post. Is she your mascot now?

Me: Yes, and your wonderful shearing of the dark weeds in my mind allowed my golden unicorn horn to grow!!![Shari's name literally means a small clearing or shearing.]

Shari: I am so glad the dark weeds have been sheared and are leaving room for growth!

As long as your golden unicorn horn is loving rather than gouging people, I'm all for it! LOL

Me: LOL. Hmmm, maybe I can set it to golden virtual hug mode...

This was followed by an eyes squeezed shut, awkward teeth smile, grimace yellow emoji reaction from Shari.

Me: Also, to be very honest, it's my way of coping with a lot of challenging situations for myself right now. My father is receiving chemo three times a week for lymphatic cancer, I cannot find my phone (missing for several days now) and of course, COVID lockdown. I would LOVE to take pictures of my children and post them on Facebook but while my phone is lost that is not a reality. In addition, my mother has asked that I keep the knowledge of my father receiving chemo three times a week from everyone but our "immediate family," i.e., my parents' children and their spouses secret. While I do not wish to dishonor her wishes, I find myself falling apart unless I turn into a strong happy unicorn.

Shari followed up on July 30, 2020.

> Shari: I am so sorry to hear about your dad. (And your lost phone.) Thank you for trusting me with that closely guarded secret. If you ever want to talk about it I am happy to listen. I believe there are times when someone else's restrictions may be okay for them but are not healthy for us. You need support to get through this! Praying that you have wisdom and a clear conscience about where to turn for the support you need (whether that is only to your husband/inside the family) or one or two trusted others.

And the following day.

> Shari: I am glad your unicorn gift has brought you such fun and joy in this hard season. I know you are regularly commenting on the reading plan [Shari's virtual Bible study]. What aspect of God's character is most meaningful to you right now?"

Me: His strength, wisdom, and love

Shari replied with a heart emoji.

I wrote the following to Brenda Jurgensmeier, the wife of one of the pastors at our church via Facebook Messenger on July 30, 2020, after I realized I needed support to deal with the potential grief of losing my father.

> Me: Dear Brenda,
> I am messaging you now because I know you have dealt with the loss of your father with grace. My father is receiving chemo three times a week for lymphatic cancer currently. I would like to pray for him, but he is so dismissive of evangelicals, with the exception of the good Ed Lovetinsky, so I do not know if he would view my Evangelical prayers as curses or bless-ings. I only know I can pray for peace and strength in my hearth and the strength to care for my husband and children while all of this is going on. How do you handle the passing of your father with grace??????
>
> Brenda: I'm sorry to hear about your father. It is never easy watching your parent go through this! I will be praying for you and for him to be saved. I'm not sure I have

great advice to share. Give yourself grace to be sad and reach out to the Father of all comfort to give you strength. Are you going to visit him? My father was only an hour away, so we made lots of trips down there.

Me: Lol, that is the hardest of all of this. He's in Wichita, KS, nine hours down South and with the boys' [our sons] and David's special food requirements* and COVID. we don't know yet if we can risk a visit. I'm trying to be a Godly unicorn in 2020 to cope with all of this …

Brenda: I'm sure that can make it emotionally harder being so far away. I'm not up on unicorns. Can you explain what that means to you?

Me: Many years ago when I worked at the Hiawatha Public Library as a page [a book shelver], I discussed with Assistant Director Pat Struttmann how excited I was to discover that there were unicorns in the Bible and how I immediately began researching what the word could or could not have meant with the language translation. In addition, my good friend

Marta Petermann gave me a toy unicorn this year for completing the adult reading program at the Hiawatha Public Library ... Once, the year I worked at the library before my youngest was born, I told Alicia and Marta that I was a unicorn (jokingly) who was going to finish an impossible task in an impossible amount of time. Sooooo ... in essence for me, unicorns mean having incredible strength in impossible situations...

Brenda: That is a good meaning. Where are they in the Bible? Are you talking about Revelation and Jesus on a white horse?

Me: King James Bible:

> Save me from the lion's mouth: for thou has heard me from the horns of the unicorns. (Psalm 22:21)

> God brought them out of Egypt; he hath, as it were, the strength of a unicorn. (Numbers 23:22)

> His glory is like the firstling of his bullock, and his horns are like the horns of the unicorns: with them he shall push the people together to the ends of the

earth: and they are the ten-thousands of Ephraim, and they are the thousands of Manasseh. (Deut. 33:17)

But my horn shalt thou exalt like the horn of the unicorn: I shall be anointed with fresh oil. (Psalm 92:10)

Canst thou bind the unicorn with his band in the furrow? Or will he harrow the valleys after thee? (Job 39:10)

All from the King James Bible, David's (my husband's) favorite translation. And, if they don't mean unicorns as we know them, they do mean oxen with incredible strength.

Brenda: Praying you will have strength. I will try to think more too about when my dad passed and e-mail you some thoughts.

After a couple hours passed, I messaged her back.

My eldest just found my phone, so that was a big help. It was missing for a couple days. Also, my good friend Alicia came out in a hot pink dress to say hi to me this morning when I dropped off extra food we had at The Little Free Pantry at the library

I patronize today. David and I just love donating anything with wheat or gluten* in it to that Little Free Pantry since it makes our burden someone else's blessing.

I ended the post with many smiley face and heart emojis.

*My husband and sons all suffer from celiac disease, which makes it unsafe for them to ingest anything with gluten (wheat, oats, barley, or rye) in it. Blessedly, it is not contagious, but it does keep us on our toes and has taught me many life lessons.

I wrote the following to Christy, a friend and fellow mother, via Facebook Messenger the morning of July 30, 2020, asking for insight on how to handle the potential passing of my father with grace:

Dear Christy,

I write to you now because I believe you handled the passing of your father with grace. Currently, my father is receiving chemo three times a week for lymphatic cancer. As he has been a very good father to me, paying for most of my college education rather than investing my grandparents' inheritance in sports, encouraging me in running Cross-Country and Track, telling me that I still had a lot of grow-ing up to do when I was in my freshman year of college and needed to seek therapy and medical aid for my anxiety issues and well, simply being there and supporting me ... Currently, my smartphone is MIA, and I cannot take loving and cute pictures of my children to post on Facebook. My mother has asked for me to keep my fa-ther's health issues and treatment secret from all of our large family but my siblings and their spouses until they decide other-wise and then a friend had the audacity to tell me that I was being too perky and inconsiderate to others with my Operation Unicorn which I'm using to cope with all of this!!!!! How do you handle the passing of your father with grace????? Thank you in advance for your insight and wonderful friendship and gorgeous heartwarming home decorations.

This was followed by many smiley faces with heart emojis alternating with the brunette lady putting her hand up as if saying, "I'm a mess, can't lie," emoji.
   Christy replied,

Oh, I am so sorry to hear about your dad. It's hard to see a parent sick. I am sure

> you are handling it as well as anyone can.
> Tell me more about your unicorn project,
> I don't know anything about it.

There was space to think and reflect on being uber polite, which Christy always is. Then she added, "I do appreciate the kind gifts."

I had dropped off a gift basket for Christmas in July, which I had crafted with yellow ribbon and little treats, like individual Kleenex packs and hand sanitizer for Christy to use in the classroom next year, when she went to work as a teacher's aide. I also dropped off an almost full box of extra baby wipes I had from buying in bulk at Target for the discount. Clorox wipes were very hard to get at the time, but baby wipes were not, and I figured Christy could use them to help clean her home or classroom.

I replied to her message:

> Lol. Once when I was really sick my father reminded me to use good sense, not necessarily common sense, but good sense. In essence, what I gathered this meant was that even though God had given me and my family unusual health issues, he had *also* given me an unusual amount of intelligence and creativity to handle them and that I should utilize the gifts God had given me to keep myself and

family healthy. In addition, ever since COVID hit, I have been in the unusual situation that I deal with complicated health issues with myself and my family daily and well and so have a stockpile of skills and enthusiasm to share with everyone (not limited to a mean management of finances, which without paying for private Christian school tuition—homeschooling due to COVID and because it's the best fit for our eldest—and trips to Kansas have left us very fiscally blessed in this period). This is my Operation Unicorn, my capability to have impossible strength in an impossible time and the way I am honoring my father while I cannot physically be present with him during his chemo battle. I chose the unicorn as my mascot as my good friend Marta Petermann gave me a toy unicorn (Uni) for completing the adult reading program at the Hiawatha Public Library this year and because I once quipped to Alicia and Marta that I was a unicorn at the library after I told them I was going to do a ridiculous amount of work in an impossible amount of time which we all knew to be impossible. Sooooo, I'm making the impossible possible and being happy to honor the sacrifices my father made for me and the wisdom he offered me. Thank you for lending an ear.

I closed with another smiley face emoji, and Christy responded with a heart emoji.

On August 3, 2020, I used Facebook Messenger to talk with my good friend Annie Jones, a fellow member of our church. She also had a parent who suffered from cancer. I changed her name to respect her privacy.

Me: Dear Annie.

Annie: Yes.

Me: I am writing to you now because I believe telling others what is going on in my life is helping me to process it in a healthy manner. Currently, my father is undergoing chemo three times a week for lymphatic cancer in Wichita, Kansas.

My mother has asked that we not tell the rest of the extended family (just us children and our spouses) until they are ready but I feel with COVID preventing us from visiting or at least, socially distancing us all so much, I need to turn to friends for support to process this and the potential that the Lord will take him as this is his second bout with Lymphatic cancer. He is 75 years old. Could you please pray for peace in my heart over this and wisdom on how to honor him and still care for my children and husband???

Annie: I'll pray. I am sorry. I was on a Barnabas call at the time you messaged. 1 Peter 5:7 "Cast your anxiety on him because he cares for you." Are you in a Barnabas?

Me: Not currently.

Annie: Maybe that would help?

Me: I agree. Do you or Brenda know of any ones open to new members???

Annie: Brenda would know. My group is full. Sorry.

Me: No, don't be, please. Thank you for letting me know to talk to Brenda!

Annie responded with a thumbs-up yellow emoji.

The following day, August 4, 2020, Annie and I continued our Messenger conversation.

Annie: You are welcome to call me or still message me as a friend.

Why doesn't your mom want your family to know? That's a huge burden for you to keep.

Me: I am not going to delve into her reasons other than to say I believe for her it makes it less real but as a thirty-five-year-old woman who listened to her mother complain that she had not been notified of an acquaintance's passing last night, I have made the adult decision to not keep it private.

[Annie inserted a yellow emoji face with frown and one tear.] Annie: I am sorry. It's hard. People are hard to understand sometimes. Is it your mom or your dad that wants to keep it private?

Me: My mother, but my father's also a very private man who's a tough guy who likes to believe he's superman even when he's not. (Sound familiar? I know I'm not unlike him.) My father being twelve years older than my mother has typically cared for her in the relationship though he would be lost without her as she handles all things social and emotional. This is the first very real instance of reverse caretaking and we are proud and happy that our mother is at least stepping up to the task and taking him to his chemo and pet scan appointments, et al.

Annie: That's good! My parents wanted to keep it private too but I encouraged them to let people know because I couldn't be there to help all the time. Plus, some people feel hurt if you don't tell them. From my standpoint, it was more that people would help if they knew and an extra hand isn't so bad to have around every now and then. It's exhausting sitting in the hospital and people tend to not eat very well or clean their house.

I wrote the following—though I did not mail it—to the Hiawatha Public Library after I was able to come terms with the realization that even if my father beat the cancer, he was seventy-five years old, this was his second bout of cancer, and even if he did beat it, he would be intellectually reduced after the battle with chemo. He sent me a USB drive to preserve the family history as he had often acted as the Hagan family historian.

Dear library folk,

I have always used my writing to sort out my dark and twisty thoughts. I love writing to you wonderful library folk because you are literary like me (I've been told I'm too intellectual by a friend from church, and I must say I adore the fact that the Hiawatha Public Library had never had a grade level with the juvenile kids section as too many people from church have gasped and said it's not right for my 11-year-old to be reading *Lord of the Rings*).

My best friend from high school, Judith Mackenzie, is now an emergency doctor in Colorado. She now has a son not too much younger than my three-year-old, and when a phenomenal group of high school girlfriends discussed getting together with our kids since all but one of us have kids now, patiently explained that since she is working as an emergency doctor and her child is in day care, the chance of her having or getting COVID are 100%, and her family (like mine) cannot risk a visit to Kansas because her parents are caring for her 90 something-year-old grandparents in their home.

Furthermore, one of us ladies, Bonnie Ice, now a specialist doctor in another state, is on Pacific time. She looks like Galadriel, played Galadriel in our Lord of the Rings Addiction Anonymous goofy videos we made in high school on New Year's Eve, and is the only one of us ladies to not yet have children.

My best college friend from this same group (Grace Potter) tried for years to conceive with her husband. When this proved fruitless, she and her husband took up foster care of infants after they downsized their home when he got a promotion and they moved. She has her master's in a form of Social Work and, after a couple of years, adopted a baby girl and later a baby boy. To boot, both Grace and her husband are Caucasian, and their beautiful children are quite obviously of at least partial African descent. How's that to battle racism with a healthy heart and love!!!!!

Grace and her husband are now farming with their two beautiful children in Kansas. It's ironic because I grew up on a farm and Grace in the suburbs.

All right, put on your dark and twisty armor. I now have the honor of telling you about Sawyer Reynolds, a middle school teacher in Kansas, who lost her first baby with her husband. Her second baby is a handsome young fellow whom I sent a small pile of books I weeded from our home library.

Sawyer is the one who instigated a reunion of all of us in August here and really wanted to get all our kids together. She lost her first child and so recognizes what a gift all children are.

All right, get your dark and twisty armor on. When we were in high school, several of us sent forks to each other as gifts or made beautiful hot-pink craft creations with them (me) and gifted them to Sawyer or others as a fun joke, sign of friendship.

All right, get your dark and twisty armor on. Last year when my father had his first cancer scare, he gave his children the real silver silverware he had inherited from his father, Dr. Frances James Hagan and his grandfather, Dr. Martin Hagan.

All right, get your dark and twisty armor on. At the time of the 1918 Spanish Flu Pandemic, Dr. Martin Hagan weighed in his opinion on whether to quarantine or not, and my good grandfather Frances James was around 4 years and 6 months old.

Now, smile, smile, smile, smile, smile, Grandpa Frances James lived until he was 80 something, taught his little brown-haired granddaughter Catherine Hagan how to mix and bake biscuits, garden (he took me to one of the many gardens he owned and maintained on a little red tractor when all the other kids abandoned me to go play) and fed me jelly beans by his sick bed when he was dying of skin cancer. He always kept a bowl of candy by his sick bed so that the little kids would come visit him.

All right, put on your I can't believe this is happening sunshine and smiles and this is serendipitous face. Martin Hagan was born and orphaned in Independence, Iowa, and because the little brown-haired granddaughter grew up into a beautiful woman who'd been taken on a "silver horse" to Iowa by her white knight of a husband to live in a magical land of goodness, my father, the eldest son of Dr. Frances James, got to visit Independence, Iowa, with me and my eldest son, taking

Martin Hagan's great-great-grandson to the place where, among other things, his great-great-great-grandparents Ned (Edward) and Mary Hagan were buried, and after a family reunion and six or more so years of life, the little brown-haired granddaughter of Frances James learned the truth about why so many of her father's side of the family were in healthcare.

Soooooo, dear readers of this tale and all folk in 2021, I do hereby knight or give thee the title of lady or lord of the fork to you all with the silver fork with a rose on its hilt and an engraved H pictured below. I do not believe in coincidences but I very much believe that Martin, like I, was a strong person in an impossible situation, and I wish to bestow upon the people of 2021 this same strength which his son Frances James and grandson James Hagan bestowed upon me through constant support and encouragement.

Sincerely,
Catherine Marie Hagan Bruno

Real sterling silver fork my father, James Hagan, gave me that was once Martin Hagan's. Please note the prairie rose on the hilt is Iowa's state flower.

I wrote to the Ladies of the Fork after they asked me what the book I was writing was about and asking for their pseudonyms, and after I shared with them all that my father was undergoing chemo three times a week for lymphatic cancer. And even if he beat the cancer, it was unlikely he would ever be at the same intellectual place he was prior to it. The Messenger conversation went like this:

> Sophia Edwards: I'm so sorry to hear that Catherine! I think it's wonderful you are writing this book and preserving your family's history.
>
> Sawyer: Agreed!! So sorry about your dad.

Me: Don't be sorry!!! He has lived an AMAZING life and the best thing I can do for him now is care for his grandsons— my sons—and honor the work he has done with our family's history!

Sophia Edwards: That's a great way to look at it, Catherine! But I'm sure it's still hard.

Me: It can be, but I've found if I don't focus on the positive the negative will take me down. I view it as part of the COVID marathon the world has assigned to me that I need to run and run well, keeping my immediate family (my husband and the boys) happy and healthy. My father and I didn't always agree on everything. He told me he would be very disappointed if I left the Catholic faith, and I converted so I could bring my husband to Christ attending a Sunday church service as a full family. He couldn't understand anything unless it was in the terms of sports. He was a very unemotional man, I felt, and it wasn't until I grew up and he took a personality test for me and we discovered he was an ISTJ, as I was, and an aunt and therapist both pointed out that we probably had trouble in our relationship because we are so much alike personality-wise that I slowly began to understand my father. Nonetheless, when I first needed to get therapeutic help for my mood disorder, he did set up the referral with our family doctor after much pleading from me, and to the best of his ability, he paid for as much of my college as he could rather than spending the inheritance from my Grandma Hagan on sports amidst other things. He also gave me the best advice I've ever gotten about how to handle my mood disorder and my family's health issues (all of the boys in my immediate family suffer from a complicated autoimmune disorder, which can only be managed through an incredibly specific diet). After I had a nervous breakdown after sipping on an energy drink for the first time ever, he told me, "Catherine, use good sense. Not necessarily *common sense* but *good sense*." What I took this to mean was that even though God had given my family and I some unique health challenges in life, he had ALSO blessed me with a unique amount of intelligence, creativity and practical capabilities and that I should use the gifts God gave me to keep myself and family happy and healthy. Thank you, wonderful ladies, for your pseudonyms.

Sophia Edwards: Life continues to be more complicated than we ever thought it would be as kids. Good for you for doing your best to make life as good as it can be.

Bea Sky: Absolutely! We look forward to reading the epic adventure!! Beautiful thoughts, hardships turned positive is the most beautiful work! I cannot wait to read it!

The following Facebook messages took place between Brenda Jurgensmeier and I on August 5, 2020, starting at 11:02 a.m.

Me: In order to emotionally process my father's health issues and the fact that even if he survives chemo he will not intellectually be the man he once was, I have written a small book about the Hagan family history and my experiences in the summer of 2020 here. I would like to credit you in it for helping me to understand what my personal definition of unicorn was and would like to preserve your privacy if you wish. Soooooo, if you wish, as a nod to our friendship, I'd like for you to choose your own fake name. If you would rather just be Brenda Jurgensmeier, I will simply leave the dedication as it is written: "To Brenda Jurgensmeier." Please let me know, and let me know your last and first names for fake name if you choose it.

Brenda: You are so kind. My name is fine.

Epilogue

In the morning of August 6, 2020, my good mother, Sharon Hagan, texted me and my five siblings that after one more doctor's visit, my father would be done with chemo and just have to do lab work from then on.

CHAPTER THREE

THE BALLAD OF THE FATHERS AND SONS

I n this chapter I share tales from Martin Hagan's life that I especially look to today, over one hundred years later, for better insight on life. Not just his but mine as well.

Note, as I am not a medical professional, I hereby disclaim any responsibility for Dr. Martin Hagan's opinions and views being treated as advice or judgement on how to handle our current COVID pandemic. I display the newspaper article to show history as it was in 1918.

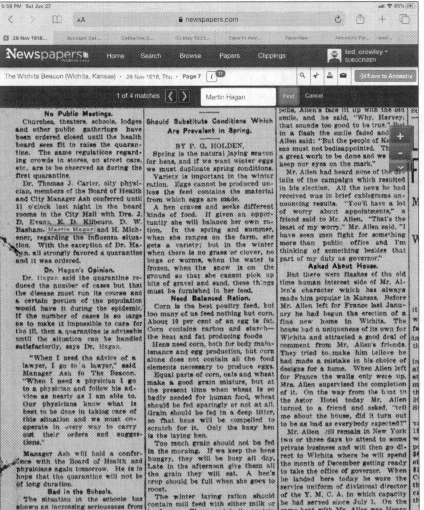

Article in the *Wichita Beacon* quoting Dr. Martin Hagan during the 1918 Spanish flu pandemic.

FRANCIS J. HAGAN, M.D.
1250 MAPLE
P.O. BOX 1837
WICHITA, KANSAS 67201
262-1087

Dear Michael;

When you have read my fathers letter to Uncle Robert you'l come to a line where he says that John went one way and he another. I am picking up at that point and tell you what he told me.

At that point someone told my dad that a Mr Mullens needed a man to work. So! off to Mullens place, when he gotthere he found that Mr Mullen had six sons and didn't need any help. However, Mullens looked at dad and said." You go six miles down the road to see a Mr Casey and don't you stop until you get there. " On the way to Caseys dad passed a farmer working on a fence. The man offered Dad a job at nineteen dollars a month. Dad told the man that Mr Mullen sent him to see Mr Casey and that he was not to stop until he got there. So off to Caseys, when he got there Mr Casey was in the pasture talking to a cattle dealer. Casey asked dad what he wanted and dad responded with he wanted a job. Mr Casey said," I do not need anyone". Dad answered you do to, Mr Mullen told me that you did. So Mr Casey told dad to go up by the barn and to sit down and wait for him. The end result was that Mr Casey hired Dad and in fact became almost a foster father figure. While at Caseys one would work in the summer and then in the winter do chores and chop wood for room and board. Other men his age were going off to school during the winter months and hence dad deceded to go to school. He went to Tilford's Academy in Vinton Iowa. It was there that he met the Kelly boys and played baseball with them and hence made a visit to the Kelly home just outside of Waterloo Iowa. That is where he met my mother. I am not sure where he got the idea of medical school. He went to the U of Iowa for two years in medicne and then transferred to Northwesten in Chicago from where he graduated.

How he got to Wichita - His senior year he had no home to go to at Xmas time so he went to work in a hospital for a Dr Sikes. Later a Dr Fabrique from Wichita went to Chicago looking for interns. He was a friend of Dr Sikes. After an interview with Fabrique. Dr Fabrique went to Sikes and asked him about this man Hagan and Sikes responded with if you don't take him I will. Hence to Wichita.

over

Dr. Frances James's letter to Mike, third-eldest son, page 1.

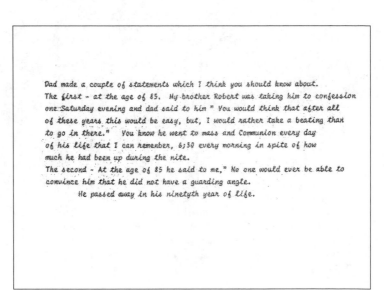

Dad made a couple of statements which I think you should know about.
The first - at the age of 85. My brother Robert was taking him to confession
one Saturday evening and dad said to him " You would think that after all
of these years this would be easy, but, I would rather take a beating than
to go in there." You know he went to mass and Communion every day
of his life that I can remember, 6:30 every morning in spite of how
much he had been up during the nite.
The second - At the age of 85 he said to me," No one would ever be able to
convince him that he did not have a guarding angle.
    He passed away in his ninetyth year of life.

Dr. Frances James's letter to Mike, third-eldest son, page 2.

MARTIN HAGAN, M. D.
SUITE 927 BEACON BLDG.
WICHITA, KANSAS

The weather here continued chilly and we had our first big frost although it was not so severe as to destroy much vegetation

A letter from Margaret says the weather has been pretty cool down in Dallas. and she is anxious to hear from you and how your are getting along. she seems to feel sorry fao you in that she was homesick at mundelein

Daniel Joseph has applied at St Louis U. medical school but we have not heard whether he has heard from them or not; a recent letter from him states that he had not.

Well I now have to make a call so I am ringing off.

With love from

Dad.

MARTIN HAGAN, M. D.
SUITE 927 BEACON BLDG.
WICHITA, KANSAS

WICHITA
SEP 27
8 ᴬᴹ
1942
KAN

1 CENT 2 CENTS

Robert McCarthy Hagan,
Campion Hall,
Campion High School,
Prairie du Chien, Wis.

Dr. Martin Hagan's letter to Robert McCarthy Hagan, his son, page 1.

MARTIN HAGAN, M. D,
SUITE 927 BEACON BLDG.
WICHITA, KANSAS

Sept. 27ᵗʰ 1942.

Dear Robert McCarthy,

I just came to the office from home. mother is typing a letter to some one. Patricia has gone to a picture show, & your little brother W.J. is resting at home.

I suppose it is hard to shake off the old homesickness entirely, I never could but mother apparently never suffered much from it, however her three younger brothers never went away from home because of homesickness.

When we were at home as a growing family I recall my father saying, after settling some of our disputes "you will come to the cross road some day & then it will be different" The time was none too long when what was left of us came to the cross road where we parted & one went one way & the other another. After the death of my mother in march 1888 & my sister in april 1888 & my father in may 1890 & my older brother in 1891. we three younger brothers were left. John was 16. I was 15 & mike was 13. mike went to an aunt at Liverpool new york. John & I stayed until march the next year, when we had a sale & sold everything. After the sale about dusk we gathered up each a little bundle of clothes & headed for the cross road only eighty rods away, he went one way & I another. We stayed at neighbors until spring opened up, about one month & then each hunted up a job on farms & got located some twenty five miles from home. That is where my homesickness began, there was no home to go back to, be the old haunts of your childhood hold out something to you. After a couple of month I had an opportunity to go back, but some how things appeared a little different, I did not fit in there exactly as I had before. I always had a longing

Dr. Martin Hagan's letter to Robert McCarthy Hagan, his son, page 2.

MARTIN HAGAN, M. D.
SUITE 937 BEACON BLDG.
WICHITA, KANSAS

Sept. 27ᵗʰ 1942.

Dear Robert McCarthy,

I just came to the office from home. Mother is typing a letter to some one. Patricia has gone to a picture show. & your little brother T.J. is resting at home.

I suppose it is hard to shake off the old homesickness entirely, I never could but mother apparently never suffered much from it however her three younger brothers never went away from home because of homesickness.

When we were at home as a growing family I recall my father saying, after settling some of our disputes " you will come to the cross road some day & then it will be different" the time was none too long when what was left of us came to the cross road where we parted & one went one way & the other another. after the death of my mother in march. 1888 & my sister in april. 1888 & my father in may 1890 & my older brother in 1891, we three younger brothers were left. John was 16. I was 15. & mike was 13. mike went to an aunt at Liverpool new york. John & I stayed until march the next year, when we had a sale & sold every-thing. after the sale about dusk we gathered up each a little bundle of clothes & headed for the cross road, only eighty rods away, he went one way & I another. he stayed at neighbors until spring opened up, about one month & then each hunted up a job on farms & got located some twenty five miles from home. That is where my homesickness began, there was no home to go back to, be the old haunts of your childhood hold out something to you, after a couple of month I had an opportunity to go back, but some how things appeared a little different, I did not fit in there exactly as I had before. I always had a longing

Dr. Martin Hagan's letter to Robert McCarthy Hagan, his son, page 3.

That spelling of your name came about in this way. one bright Sunday afternoon you were taken to the cathedral to be baptized Dr. & Mrs Roberts being your sponsers, Father Mangon officiating. He asked me what the name. I said Robert McCarty Hagan, whereupon He wrote down Robert McCarthy Hagan, I noticed the writing but said nothing. Dr Roberts called my attention to it but I thought it made little difference. so it would little good to dig up the bones of my uncle Moses because whether his name was McCarty, or McCarthy, the baptismal record shows McCarthy. Uncle Moses was unfortunate in having no home when he was a young man. contracted tuberculosis & finding himself ill went to his sisters home. where he died some time about my early childhood, no doubt he brought tuberculosis into the family from which my sister & two brothers died, the first one in 1885 second in 1888 & the third in 1891.

Top this one. a man went into a restuaunt and said to the waitress. "Bring me some burned toast, some very greasy bacon with fried eggs cold, some hot or warm orange juice, some coffee burned, muddy but not hot." In due time the waitress returned & said here is you your greasy bacon with fried eggs, your cold muddy coffee, your warm orange juice & burned toast He said that is fine, now sit down and nag me I am home-sick.

Freddie is alright, he needs none of that tapping on the head but lots of hamburgers. Mother got sympathetic the other evening & decided to give Freddie a nice bone & a hunk of fat. but took him to the garage to give it to him & as she opened the garage door, it being dark there, something come on had the bone, grabbed the bone out of her hand and freddie got the fat —

Dr. Martin Hagan's letter to son Robert McCarthy Hagan, page 4.

MARTIN HAGAN, M. D.
SUITE 927 BEACON BLDG.
WICHITA, KANSAS

The weather here continues chilly and we had our first big frost although it was not so severe as to destroy much vegetation

A letter from Margaret says the weather has been pretty cool down in Dallas, and she is anxious to heare from you and how your are getting along, she seems to feel sorry fao your in that she was homesick at Mundelein

Daniel Joseph has applied at St. Louis U. medical school but we have not heard whether he has heard from them or not; a recent letter from him states that he had not.

Well I now have to make a call so I am ringing off.

With love from

Dad.

MARTIN HAGAN, M. D.
SUITE 927 BEACON BLDG.
WICHITA, KANSAS

WICHITA
SEP 27
8 PM
1942
KANS

Robert McCarthy Hagan,
Campion Hall,
Campion High School,
Prairie du Chien. Wis.

Dr. Martin Hagan's letter to son Robert McCarthy Hagan, last page and front of envelope.

Martin and Kathryn Hagan family photo taken in Wichita, Kansas.

CHAPTER **FOUR**

GRACE IN UNEXPECTED PLACES

Grace, like a volunteer plant, can show
up in the most unexpected places.

Only a derecho can turn cancer into a good thing. Such was the case on August 10, 2020. A derecho, a combination of thunderstorms and straight-line winds, essentially an inland hurricane, hit Iowa at noon or so. Our Bruno household was without electric power for six days. Our saving grace was the gas generator Papa Hagan had mailed us at the beginning of COVID lockdown. In an attempt to clear our garage for the second car my husband and I were finally purchasing, we considered getting rid of it. But Papa Hagan was dying of cancer, so we felt we couldn't.

During the week of August 10, 2020, grace showed

up in the most unexpected of places amid a natural disaster. A kind neighbor shared his generator with us when we couldn't get ours to start. A professional chef in our neighborhood gave us wonderfully seasoned ribs from his hotel workplace, which was going to have to toss the food if it wasn't eaten because the electricity was out and the refrigeration to keep the food good wasn't working.

A week after the derecho hit, I closed the book deal on *Operation Unicorn: Making Possible the Impossible* with Simon and Schuster's Archway Publishing division. Because my good friend Christy had said on Facebook to keep checking with anyone we knew in the area to make sure they were safe because the derecho damage had been so erratic, among many other unexpected graces, I was able to add Brenda Powers, the Hiawatha Public Library board president, to a Facebook derecho resource page. I also noted library friends in Iowa and where they were working post-derecho. I praised God those two were safe and well.

Initially after the storm had passed, my husband let me know that we would have to help our neighbors in spite of COVID restrictions because of how bad the damage had been. I did not fully understand what he meant until I looked at the street outside our front door. The entire street was blocked by tree limbs everywhere. My good husband, survivalist that he is, popped on a yellow hard hat, grabbed our garden shears, and went to clear the roads with other male neighbors. After he had worked awhile, he told me to have our eldest watch our youngest and to come help clear the roads and the neighbors' driveway. I put on a unicorn charm I had gotten in the mail on Saturday for emotional strength, put on shoes and a hat, and played Rosie the Riveter unicorn post-derecho. Mr. Bruno did not just marry me for my good looks. He knows I'm an able-bodied woman.

As the afternoon progressed, we realized we would not have electricity that night. The storm had hit at twelve o'clock or so. A young ginger-haired boy rode up on his bicycle to let us know there was an electricity source where we could charge our phones at the end of a cul-de-sac in the neighborhood. I finished some wood chopping, communicated where I was going to my husband, and then took both our cell phones to get them charged.

As I walked to the end of the cul-de-sac, neighbors walked with me. Sometimes people walk great distances or wait in long lines for water, food, or toilet paper. On the night of August 10, 2020, in our neighborhood we walked and waited in line for electricity. The father of the boy who had notified us about the electricity with his sister, had called the company he worked for because they had given him a truck that produced its own electricity for his work with them. In light of our neighborhood's current situation, he asked his company if he could borrow the truck so his neighborhood could charge their phones. Blessedly, his company obliged, and our neighborhood had another resource to help recovery after our latest natural disaster.

Sick of isolation from months of COVID lockdown restrictions, our neighbors all happily chatted and did what we could to help each other. A woman who worked for the electric company let us know when she thought electricity might be restored. Everyone who knew about the situation checked in with a woman who was on call as a caregiver and could only get her phone charged to 15 percent before she had to go to work. The wife of the man who provided the electricity was an old friend of mine, and I was happy to catch up with her. We both talked about what we hoped our children would be able to do for school for the autumn semester of 2020. It was every parent's million-dollar question.

As the week progressed, my in-laws were able to drive to Iowa on Wednesday, August 12 and take the kids back to their home in Kansas the following day. I let my mother-in-law know that my father was under care for cancer so that she knew if my mother couldn't take the kids, it was not because she was being mean but because she was not in a position to do so because of taking care of my father. At my husband's request, my in-laws had brought sushi for dinner on Tuesday night and several resources, such as gas. My father-in-law even joined my mother-in-law on the trip as he was so sick of not traveling due to COVID restrictions or cautions. We were all so thrilled to see family alive and well. As my mother-in-law drove off in her van with the grandkids in the back, she shot me a happy grin. She'd managed to get our kids for a little bit of the summer after all.

As the days passed, my husband and I reset our clocks to the rising and setting sun. Sunlight was our only light besides flashlights, our phones, and candles. Blessedly, we still had working water. We grilled and used a campfire oven my husband had to cook our food. We had plenty of clean clothes when the derecho hit August 10, and with the children in Kansas, I didn't have to handwash a load of laundry until Saturday, August 15.

We helped our neighbors clear debris from their yards and worked to get all our tree debris to the curb in front of the sidewalk. Trash, recycling, and yard pick up did not even come on their normal days that week; the city was so overwhelmed. Residents were instructed not to call police officers unless it was an absolute emergency as they were so overwhelmed. When we tried to get our garage door open with the generator—Thursday, I believe it was it took a rush on the generator and unplugging our refrigerator and freezer that we had plugged into the generator to keep our food from spoiling. Blessedly, I was able to get it open. I then drove the car around to check on friends in town to make sure they were coming out all right.

The husband of my good friend Regan Smetz told me their family was making out fine. They were just trying to saw down trees. They had family in town, and he did not believe that their immediate family would need to file an insurance claim. Their family, like ours, had made it out of this natural disaster on the upside. I visited an old friend in Hiawatha and made certain that she was doing fine. The old friend smiled at me and was happy to hear from me.

As the week progressed, I dropped off load after load of diapers and wipes to the Big Brothers and Big Sisters of Cedar Rapids. They were running operations out of a home in Hiawatha because their building was unfunctional due to derecho damage.

My friend Marty Ramirez is a down-to-earth chef who served hundreds to thousands of meals to people via Operation Barbecue Relief. Because Marty is a dependable, community-oriented guy, I asked him if I could drop off water bottle donations at his home for the effort. Marty said yes, and I used my Iowa muscle to deliver several packages of water bottles and some crackers and granola bars. Marty got them where they needed to go. Once again I am proud and happy to have the Ramirez family as friends. I very much hope that I will be able to get his wife, Barbara, and youngest daughter, Jazmin, to attend our church's Christmas Women's Social in 2020—God and COVID regulations allowing. I would so love to catch up with the Ramirez ladies and hear what their family has been up to.

My husband and I finally came into the possession of our new Subaru Cross-Trek, which we bought pre-derecho. The car reminded me of *Baby Shark* before we put on the luggage rack (a favorite cartoon of my toddler's, and a current huge hit among toddlers). It was a comfort to us when we drove to the covered bridges in Madison County to pick up the kids from Kansas.

We had sent the kids to Kansas one or two days post-derecho when we realized we didn't know when our electricity would be restored. It was restored six days post-derecho, on Sunday. I wrote a check to tithe for derecho relief for our church while in our car. My husband noticed the neighbors' lights were on. He stopped the car and checked ours. I danced and cried in front of our garage door in relief when I saw we had electric power again. Throughout the Cedar Rapids, Marion, and Hiawatha metropolitan areas, electric power outage was such that people began calling the workers who arrived in the white trucks with cranes to fix it ice-cream trucks because of the absolute joy it gave us when our electric power was restored.

Our entire local area worked on getting the word out to people outside of the derecho path and outside of Iowa about how bad our derecho damage and cleanup were. We all knew if we didn't advocate for ourselves, our local area would drown. I helped clear tree debris from neighbors' yards and our own and physically labored until my bones and muscles hurt. In the first few days, I just knew. The damage the derecho left was so severe that no one person could clean it up. We needed to work together. And we needed outside aid.

As our community continues to recover from the derecho, I have found I have new levels of feeling blessed. Our household has working electricity. There are many in the area the derecho hit that still do not have electricity. More than one friend has had a tree fall on to their house or are still waiting and praying for insurance companies to accurately assess the damage that was done their homes. Friends ask others to pray that their insurance companies are accurate in assessing whether their living areas will be safe to repair after a tree or trees have broken the roofs and/or ceilings of their homes. Insurance companies will not cover debris removal unless the debris is physically on the house.

As I drive throughout Cedar Rapids, Hiawatha, and Marion, I still see many churches and buildings without roofs or with tarps. Large trees are still positioned sideways as the derecho had smacked them into buildings. Stop signs, street signs, and even large billboard-style signs on metal poles have been leveled by derecho winds. The Marion Public Library, which had hoped to open their doors to the public again—with several COVID safety measures—had its building condemned as a result of derecho damage. At Thomas Park in Marion just yesterday, I met a father who had also attended Music and Movement at the Marion Library with his child or children. He had not yet heard the building was condemned and was greatly saddened to hear the news. My friend Amy, who grew up with the Marion Library as her home library, was greatly saddened as well. As a mother, I already miss the fact that the library, with a beautiful painted wooden boat and train-style shelving that held the toddler books with padded chairs in between, no longer exists.

By the grace of God, the Hiawatha Public Library building still stands tall and strong and proud, and the librarians are working on moving into the new part of their recently built building. On August 6, 2020, I had complained to the Ladies of the Fork that it seemed God always gave me more challenging experiences than others. I believe teaching, particularly in a one-on-one or small group setting, is one of the gifts He gave me, and though I grow constantly frustrated by the challenges He sends my way, I take comfort and courage in the fact that Martin Hagan struggled as much if not more than I do and rose to the challenge. I reread my rough draft of *Operation Unicorn: Making Possible the Impossible* and retaught myself a lesson on courage and strength of character and perseverance via remembering Martin's experiences in Iowa over a hundred years ago.

As I researched Martin Hagan's tales and then put the Hagan family history documents in order for the first section of this book, I came across a comment of Martin Hagan's. When his son Robert McCarthy Hagan, known to me as Big Bobby or Uncle Bobby, took him to Catholic confession when he was too old to go by himself, Martin told him that no matter how old he got, it never got easier. God, or our conscience, can be absolutely terrifying. If I did not face Him in all honesty, however, and publish this book I strongly believe God wants me to publish, I do not believe I could sit in front of Christ when my time comes and be able to face Him and honestly say I have followed the incredible examples of strength of character my great-grandfather Martin Hagan and his grandson, James Hagan, set for me. Martin through his examples, and James through his meticulous work on our family's history, the organization and depth of which I am still benefiting from as I finish writing this book.

As I read and prepared the letters of Martin Hagan for publication, I learned Edward Hagan was shy like me. Sensitive people, according to the personality books I have read, are best suited as parents. I had considered working to eradicate the sensitive side of my personality when I first started therapy for my mood disorder; I had gathered it was causing more harm than good. The books I read, however, said that sensitives made good parents and I wanted children some day, so I kept it. God has rewarded me with children.

As time passed post-derecho, and while the children were still away from home, I had ordered a small wallet card from Personalization Mall with the personalization, "In honor of Edward Hagan, a poor Irish farmer who had the good sense to love his son, I return the love to Iowa today." I needed to remember why I kept on going and doing good.

One evening, stressed from everything about the post-derecho cleanup, I snapped at my husband. I had on a green dress and red jewelry I had meant to gift to a friend but chose to wear that day for post-derecho confidence. Jacque was helping me understand via Facebook that I needed to take as good care of myself as I did of others. Blessedly, as I left the house to cool down via a walk, I opened the mailbox and discovered the metal card had been delivered. I took it with me to go meditate down by the creek at end of our street. The creek bed was dry when I got there, but there were still many trees tall, proud, and beautiful around it. I sat on a fallen log and prayed to my God to find the strength to love in Iowa during this challenging time.

As I was meditating and praying, a group of neighborhood boys discovered me by the creek. I laughed. "You didn't expect to find me here," I said. They were confused but didn't know whether to come down to the creek or not. I told them, "It's dry. Go check it." For the first time ever, this group of neighborhood boys actually did what I asked them to do. They looked in the creek bed and it was dry. They looked back at me.

"You want to hear a good story?" I asked. I asked them where they thought my great-grandfather was from.

They replied, "Kansas!" The word had gotten out that my immediate family was from Kansas as one of the boys had attended my eldest's third birthday party when he was much younger.

I laughed and said, "No, Iowa. He was born in Independence, Iowa, about an hour and a half from where we are now. Would you like to hear what happened to him and how it relates to our current COVID pandemic?"

The boys looked at me curiously. I explained, "He was orphaned when he was a young boy not much older than yourselves. He walked down the road alone but alive and had two choices—to either work for a farmer who would pay him a lot of money or to go work for John Casey as his father had asked him to. Which do you think he chose?"

"The money, of course," said the orneriest of the boys.

"No," I said. "Everyone always thinks it is about the money. He went to work for John Casey. Do you think John Casey wanted Martin to work for him?"

"No," the orneriest of the boys said.

"You're right! Martin was a nobody, a nothing, an orphan, and trouble John Casey didn't want to deal with. How do you think Martin got John Casey to accept him?"

The boys couldn't figure it out, so I continued, "Martin, like me, was a sweet-talker, and he talked John Casey or his wife into it. What do you think happened to Martin over the years?"

The boys were clueless. "He either enlisted or was

drafted for the Spanish-American War. I do not know which one but hope to learn through researching my family history more."

Then I asked the boys, "What do you think happened to Martin after the war?"

The boys asked, "Did he die?"

"No, he survived and went to the University of Iowa. Later he went to a university in Chicago to become a doctor and to fight headfirst the devil that had taken so much from him. Both he and his brother John became doctors. I do know not know what happened to the third son."

The boys continued looking at me curiously. I told them some more tales.

"In 1918, during the Spanish flu pandemic, my great-grandfather Martin Hagan made a comment in the *Wichita Beacon* about whether to quarantine people during the pandemic in Wichita, Kansas. Listening to me speak so much now, how long do you think his comment was? Was it short, or a yay or nay? Listening to me speak now, how long do you think it was?"

"Long," answered the eldest of the boys, who had been to my eldest's third birthday party.

"Correct," I said. "There was a small board of doctors, and they all said, 'Yay to quarantine.' All these doctors got one paragraph all together. Martin Hagan, as longwinded as I, spoke a full paragraph. I cannot remember exactly what it said. It was against the quarantine at the time but not against the quarantine in the future should certain conditions prevail."

Then I told them about my aunt Corinne, Martin's granddaughter. "She married an orthopedic surgeon. Do you know what her husband's father's profession was?"

"No," the boys replied.

"A mailman," I honestly answered. "When my uncle Jim Kelly asked her to marry him, do you think she wanted a diamond ring?" I asked.

"Of course!" the boys said. "All girls want diamonds."

I laughed. "She did not! She told him, 'All girls get diamonds. I want to be different. I want an emerald.' What do you think he told her? Knowing she was a great catch, so to speak—like me—and worried other men might attempt to steal her if they didn't know she was his, what do you think he told her?"

The boys looked at me, their faces blank. They had no idea.

"He told her he wanted a diamond ring for her. Then she explained what shade of green the emerald must be. What shade of green do you think her emerald is? What shades of green are there?"

The boys answer, "Uh, verde?"

"No," I answer. "Think harder!" The boys stare at me totally enthralled.

"Kelly green," I explain. "Kelly, like his last name, so that everyone will always know she is his."

"Did my aunt Corinne get boys or girls when they had children for loving him so well?" I asked the boys.

They looked at me blankly.

"She had four children for loving him so well," I tell them. "They were all of one gender. Were they boys or girls?" I ask them.

The boys look at me blankly but with full attention.

"I can tell you she wanted at least one other gender of child and finally has a granddaughter. So based on that, are all her children boys or girls?"

"Boys!" they finally answer.

"Yes! Just like the new nephew my husband and I were happy to hear about in August 2020. It seems to be another year for boys. I sent our nephew's mother a pink sparkly necklace while she was pregnant in the hope that we would get another girl, but it does seem 2020 is a year for the boys here."

The boys kept looking at me, entranced by my stories, so I continued. "My great-grandfather had one son who died as an infant. What do you think his name was? Given that my great-grandfather's father, Edward Hagan, died before he was an old man but as an adult, what do you think the name of the infant son was who perished?"

"Edward Hagan," the orneriest answered.

"Correct!" I answered. "What do you think happened to the Edward Hagan of my father's generation, my uncle Ned?"

"He died!" they all answered.

I laughed. "He did not. He is alive and well today, a happy old man who never let me lose at checkers when I was a kid, used the cow's udders to shoot milk at cats and kittens when it was his chore to milk on my grandparents' farm, and taught me how to have fun no matter what job I was doing."

"Go on now," I told the boys. I am tired from talking so much and need my alone time to breathe and recoup."

I thanked God for answering my prayer. Earlier in the summer, I had kept bugging this same group of neighborhood boys about not wearing helmets while they were riding their bikes all over our neighborhood. I had even bought helmets for them and placed them by the sidewalk where they rode and let the boys know they were theirs for the taking if they so wished and it was okay with their parents.

To my horror, the boys not only turned down the helmets but the orneriest made fun of my three-year-old for not wearing a helmet when he ran out on his tricycle without a helmet before I could catch him.

I will not write what I told the boys to behave after that here, but suffice it to say it was not something I would not say in a classroom. And it got them to quickly run away every time I drove our car out of the driveway, and they have not bothered my three-year-old since.

After that confrontation, I let the boys know I had worked as a substitute teacher and was bothering them about their helmets, not because I wanted to pick on them, but because I cared about them and wanted to know they were safe. "You hear me?" I said as I looked directly into the orneriest one's eyes and explained it.

The eldest, after or before that confrontation, rode through our neighborhood streets with his father, both without helmets. All boys and father made it safely through the derecho. Desperate for manpower post-derecho, I even asked the orneriest of the boys for help cleaning up the tree debris. I told him I would pay him in cash. He would need to wear a face mask, and I would need a signed permission slip from his guardian or guardians. He listened to my offer, opted not to take it, and rode down the sidewalk on his bike, continuing to use a cell phone for entertainment or to take pictures of the derecho damage. The fact that I still yelled, "Stay safe!" after him though he refused my offer, startled him. Dorothy Stegman, my incredibly tough high school English teacher, had once cried in front of the class about one of her former students, who had died bungee jumping. The fact that tough-as-nails Mrs. Stegman had cried stuck with me. I paid forward what she had taught me about teaching kids that day.

In the days following the derecho and before our kids came home, I received a card in the mail from this same English teacher. She was currently teaching high school English again at my old high school. The card was light blue with white edging around it, and the following was written in white:

Courage is
Resistance to fear,
Mastery of fear,
Not absence of fear

On the inside, Dorothy wrote,

Catherine—Aug. 11,

You must think ill of your old teacher as your letters came to school in June, but I did not arrive until this week! It was a lovely surprise to get these notes from you with such kind thoughts! Thank you for the Starbucks gift card as well. I will certainly use it as the school year begins—an unusual one, for sure!

Dot Stegman

On the beautiful creek with trees on the sides nature envelope, she had written when she sealed the letter, "P.S. I *loved* the Kipling quote!"

I had written to her a slightly changed version of the Rudyard Kipling poem I had memorized as a freshman in high school English:

O East is East, and West is West,
And never the twain shall meet

Til earth and sky stand presently
Before God's great judgment seat.

But there is neither East nor West,
Border nor breed nor birth
When two strong *women*
Stand face-to-face
Though they come from the ends of the
earth.

On August 16, 2020, I posted a picture I took that day of me wearing my, "Out the Door in '04" Kapaun class graduation high school T-shirt and matching blue eye shadow. I had a large smile on my face. I wrote,

> I like to believe I did our '04 class honor today when I dropped off 2 packages of water bottles, cold Cokes and zip lock bags to Linn County Public Health in Cedar Rapids, IA #DERECHO RELIEF

Sawyer Reynolds commented, "I remember that shirt! You are awesome!!!" I hit like.

Sally Kaley commented, "It's a KMC kinda day!" She posted a pic of herself with a shirt with an outlined cross and KMC in the left corner of the cross, and SADD was in the top-right corner of the cross. In the bottom left corners of the cross were '03 and '04, respectively.

David Smelts wrote, "Pretty sure I've only got my track sweatpants left at this point."

To which I replied, "David Smelts donate to Cedar Rapids Derecho Relief, and I'll happily mail the shirt." I added the brunette in an orange shirt with hands up saying, "Can't lie. I'm a mess" gesture and a purple heart emoji before adding, "Please!!!"

On August 15, 2020, I sent a Facebook message to my friend Sally Smith: "Sally, are you all safe over where you live???"

> Sally: Electricity came on today after being off since Monday. We were lucky we had water, even hot water. We had golf ball–size hail in April with several properties where we live having shingle damage, so new shingles, or we would have been in sad shape. Lost lots of trees. Our daughter is in her third day of intensive care with COVID-19. This has not been a good year.

> Me: Virtual hugs to you friend. Know you are in my prayers [I inserted a praying emoji and a red heart with a red bead underneath it], and I feel very blessed to have such a strong Iowan woman for a friend.

> Sally: "Thank you very much."

Sally sent me an update on Facebook on August 24, 2020:

> Harry, my son-in-law, called at 6 a.m. My daughter has pneumonia and she is back in the ICU to be intubated. Harry said he was going to see her no matter what. He would suit up. He is trying to get there from work in Tama before she is intubated. Harry got to see her for three minutes and talked to the doctor. He said she looked good and talked to him through a mask. They are having trouble putting in a PICC line in her blood as it is so thick. They are worried about clots. She was asleep for a few days. A nurse called. They got PICC lines in and ventilator on. Been roller-coaster ride. We must stay hopeful.

She ended her message with a yellow emoji face with a frown and a tear falling from one eye.

I sent Jacque a Facebook message on August 23, 2020, regarding my book:

> Me: Hi Jacque,
> As a healthy way of processing the events I have lived through this summer I wrote *Operation Unicorn* and am now publishing it through Simon and Schuster. I might,

however, be below the minimum page requirement. With your permission, may I use some of our Facebook Messaging here to pad up my book with Goodwill???? I can give you a pseudonym (fake name) to protect you and your family's privacy. Perks, you get to pick your own name [smiley face emoji]. Please let me know and thank you either way!

Jacque: Sure!

Me: What do you want your name to be????

Jacque: Hmmmm ... let me think about it!! I also have one other story for you to add.

Me: What's your other story???

When I hadn't received a reply, I sent her another message on August 26, 2020:

Me: Jacque, what's your other story??? Also, brave woman, I've put in italics that you survived the '08 flood too and so I knew you were a good, wise woman more experienced than I to turn to for insight on how to survive challenging circumstances with love and dignity (you're a great mother to your children and wife to your husband).

Jacque: Thank you for all the kind words and "surprises" you have given me over the last couple of months! So, my other story is sitting in front of your door! This is a wandering Jew plant. I took the runners that fell off my plants hanging on my front porch during the derecho storm. I took those runners and planted them in pots to give to my friends! [heart emoji] I hope you enjoy it! Thank you!

She closed with a yellow face emoji with one eye closed giving a small red heart side-mouth smooch.

Sitting on my porch was a gorgeous dark-green plant with dark-purple and then lighter purple blooming forth from the center of its leaves. I had foolishly thought it was a neighborhood friend who I had "Christmased in July" with gifts who had dropped it off when the doorbell rang and my eldest child came to get me to let me know someone had been at our door. Jacque's incredible heart again brought me to tears. This woman inspires me never to stop caring for others, to set boundaries so that I do not overwhelm myself, and to care for myself as well as I care for others. And well, it just makes me incredibly happy that we live within reasonably short driving distance of each other.

Also on August 26, I posted,

> Derecho recovery unexpected side effect, I keep washing the dishes by hand and putting them in the dish drainer rather than using the dishwasher even though we have electricity ... Is anyone else behaving differently with electricity back?????

It was liked by my father-in-law.

CHAPTER **FIVE**

SPROUTS OF RECOVERY

The following was written by my friend Shari in a smiling sun thank you card sent to me post-derecho for the goodies and kind gifts I had unicorn dropped on her front porch and then rang the doorbell and ran off. Her daughter Mary picked up the gift bag, and for at least a week, until they opened and found the card inside, they could not figure out whether the gift bag was for Shari or Mary.

> "A generous person will prosper; whoever refreshes others will be refreshed." (Proverbs 11:25)

Catherine—

Just wanted to say thank you for the mail, gifts, and posts you have sent me since

COVID started. I have been greatly encouraged by your generosity and love.
Sorry it took me so long to say it to you.

Shari

Shari had already sent a thank you note for the sparkly gift bag on their porch, but this was the first note
thanking me for mail and Facebook encouragement
posts.

Brenda Jurgensmeier wrote this post-derecho after
I left a bag with soap, a bath bomb, and bath brushes
in it for a, "self-spa event after a day of physical la-
bor cleaning up the derecho tree, house debris." The
Jurgensmeiers' home was unlivable post-derecho. They
still had a pile of debris they pulled out from it in front
of their house on Sunday, August 30, 2020. Brenda
had been asking on Facebook for, among other things,
a portable clothes rack to save some of their clothing.

Catherine,

Thank you so much for the gift of soaps
and other goodies. Your kindness and
thoughtfulness are very much appreciated.
I hope that you have been staying encouraged with everything that has been
going on, especially with your father's
health issues.

Your heavenly father is always there and will be the constant stability even when your father cannot be.

"I keep my eyes always on the Lord. With Him at my right hand, I will not be shaken." (Psalm 16:8)

He is standing right next to you, holding your hand through it all!

Love in Christ,
Brenda

When I first started attending the same church as the Jurgensmeiers, I had once stated to a woman at a women's social time that I had trouble taking the Bible seriously due to media influence and personal influence in my upbringing. Brenda called me out on this when I asked if she could set me up with a Barnabas group. I shared with her one of my personal horror stories, physical abuse when I was sixteen years old by a woman who had been a religious teacher at the private religious high school my parents had sent me to. Brenda then set me up with PC counseling in which I learned more life lessons and blessedly, took the Bible seriously enough to be able to understand what it meant when it mentioned unicorns.

Sally Smith updated me on her daughter on September 10, 2020 in the following Facebook post:

Happy to hear my daughter moved from ICU to Pulmonary today, Thursday, September 10, 2020. You may send cards, flower, etc. to Tami Fuller at St. Luke's Hospital.

I sent Tami a bright, colorful card with my message written inside:

Hi Tami,

I am a 35-year-old woman who is friends with your mother. Back in 2016 I was hospitalized for post-partum issues for a birth in September. I am alive and well today. If I can get through that, you can get through this!!! Happy to hear you made it to Pulmonary!!! You are a Warrior Woman!!! You go girl!!!

Catherine Bruno

On September 12, 2020, I googled Marion Public Library board minutes to see what the Marion Library had or had not been up to post-derecho. Their building had been destroyed, and I was curious about what had happened since. To my delight, I discovered that they were open at a new location in Marion and had "things" that patrons could check out, including a binocular set with books of Iowa birds in it. I called the library to place the kit on hold that day. What a joy to be able to check out clear activity kit packs for my children again. And what an absolute joy that the Marion Library figured out a way to reopen so soon after the derecho destroyed their building.

If you want to help the area recover from the devastation of the derecho, there are places to donate to or volunteer at that will help people who have harder lives because the derecho hit Iowa:

Iowa Derecho Storm Resource Center
1150 27th Ave SW
Cedar Rapids, IA 52404
(319)432-9754
togetherweachieve.org

HACAP
1515 Hawkeye Drive
Hiawatha, IA 52233
319-393-7811

Catherine McCauley Center
1220 5th Ave. SE
Cedar Rapids, IA 52403
319-363-4993

Willis Dady Homeless Shelter
1247 4th Ave. SE
Cedar Rapids, IA
319-362-7555

Family Promise of Linn County
610 31st SE
Cedar Rapids, IA
319-540-6494

Linn County Public Health
1020 6th St. SE
Cedar Rapids, IA 52401
319-892-6000

Marion Public Library Foundation
Donate via PayPal via the Marion
Public Library website,
marionpubliclibrary.org.
(Please make sure it is the Marion, *Iowa*,
public library website you are on.)

Samaritan's Purse
www.samaritanspurse.org

ABOUT THE AUTHOR

Catherine Bruno is a stay-at-home mom who loves her kids, husband, and the family cat.

Printed in the United States
by Baker & Taylor Publisher Services